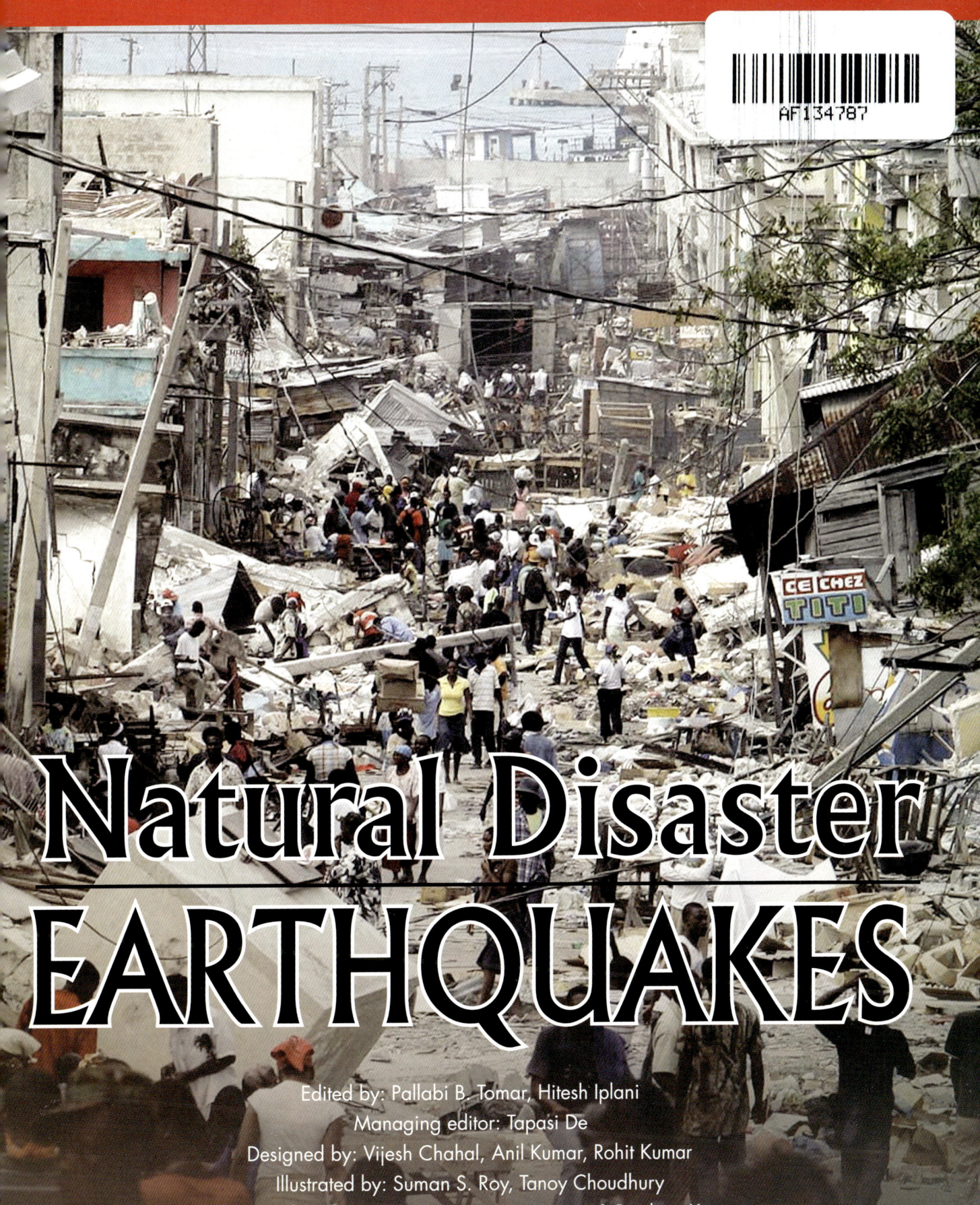

PEGASUS ENCYCLOPEDIA LIBRARY

Natural Disaster
EARTHQUAKES

Edited by: Pallabi B. Tomar, Hitesh Iplani
Managing editor: Tapasi De
Designed by: Vijesh Chahal, Anil Kumar, Rohit Kumar
Illustrated by: Suman S. Roy, Tanoy Choudhury
Colouring done by: Vinay Kumar, Kiran Kumari & Pradeep Kumar

CONTENTS

What is an earthquake? 3

What causes an earthquake? 4

Where do earthquakes occur? 6

What is a fault? 7

Types of earthquakes 9

Aftershocks 11

Seismic waves 12

How are earthquakes measured? 13

Relation between earthquakes and volcanoes 15

Effects of earthquakes 16

Earthquakes and animals 19

Better safe than sorry 20

Some deadly earthquakes 21

Test Your Memory 31

Index 32

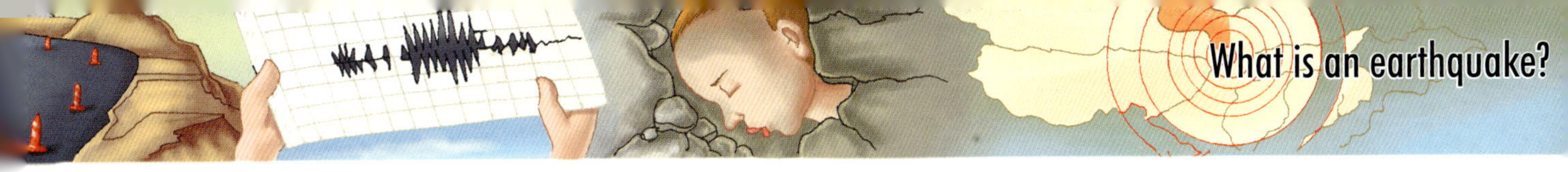

What is an earthquake?

Earthquakes are one of the most powerful natural forces on earth and which regularly affect people around the world. Like hurricanes and tornadoes, earthquakes can hit at anytime and are equally damaging.

An earthquake is the shaking of the ground caused by the sudden breaking and movement of large sections (tectonic plates) of the earth's rocky outermost crust. The edges of the tectonic plates are marked by faults (or fractures). Most earthquakes occur along the fault lines when the plates slide past each other or collide against each other.

As the Earth's plates move, the rocks in the crust gets pushed and pulled, scraped and jostled. Over time, pressure slowly builds up inside the rocks. When they can't take the pressure anymore, the rocks suddenly crack and shift. Their movement releases waves of energy called an earthquake.

The ground shakes up and down and from side to side as energy waves or vibrations, radiate in every direction. Earthquakes can tear through streets and destroy buildings that are not well built.

Earthquakes strike suddenly, violently, and without warning at any time of the year and at any time of the day or night.

EARTHQUAKES

What causes an earthquake?

As the earth's crust is made up of numerous segments or 'plates' that are constantly moving slowly, vibrations can occur and result in small earthquakes. Most earthquakes are quite small but are not readily felt. Larger and more violent earthquakes are those that occur when there is a release of energy as the plates slide past or collide into one another.

Earthquakes are caused due to two major reasons.

Plate tectonic theory

The earth is made up of four main layers. The outermost layer is the crust, then the mantle, the outer core and at the centre of the earth the inner core.

The crust is made up of hard rock, mainly granite. The mantle is mainly molten lava on which the crust is floating. The core is mostly iron, with the outer core being liquid and the inner being solid. The mantle is continually moving; this is called convection.

Astonishing fact

Alaska has the highest number of earthquakes than any other state in US.

The earth is divided into more than a dozen plates, which are floating on the mantle. This theory is called plate tectonics. The plates often rub together, pull apart, collide or dive under one another. These movements cause earthquakes and also volcanoes.

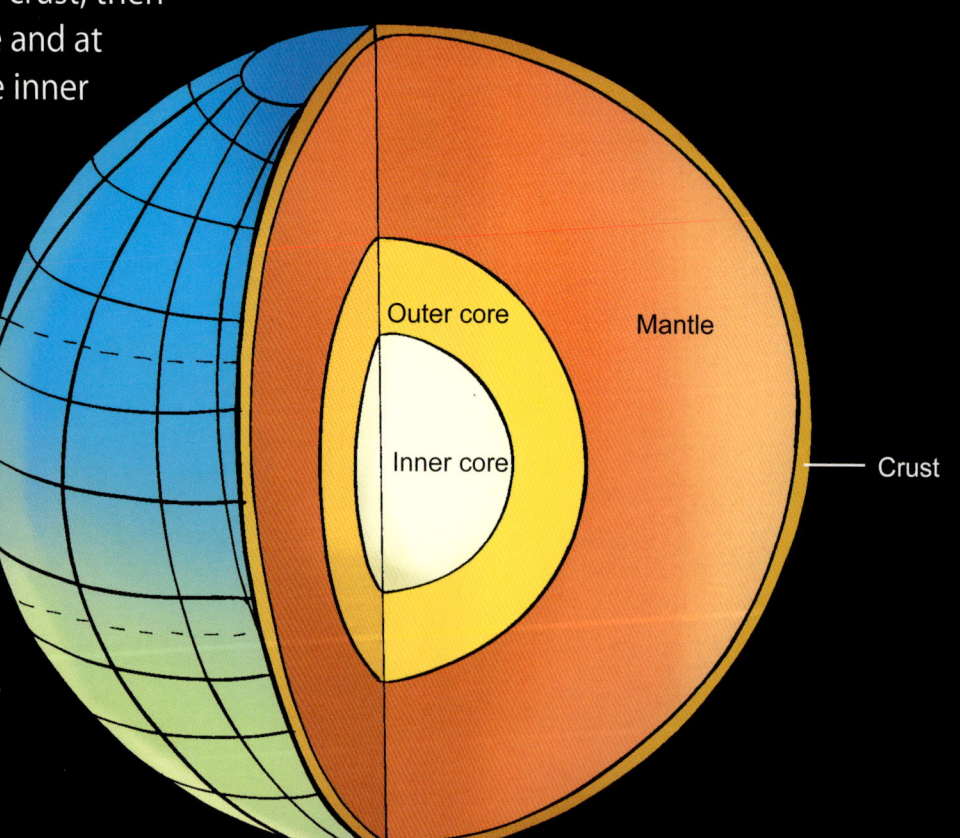

Volcanic eruptions

When volcanoes erupt, it is because the molten magma under the crust of the earth is under enormous pressure. And to release that pressure it looks for an opening and exerts pressure on the earth's crust and the plate in turn. A place, which is the seat of an active volcano, is often prone to earthquakes as well because when the pressure that is exerted by the magma exceeds the limit, these plates move causing earthquakes.

Earthquakes are also caused after a volcanic eruption since the eruption also leads to a disturbance in the position of plates, which either moves further or resettle which can result into severe or light tremors.

The excessive exploitation of earth's resources for our own benefits like building dams to store large volumes of water and blasting rocks and mountains to build bridges and roads is also the reason behind such natural disruptions.

A typical earthquake lasts under 60 seconds.

Where do earthquakes occur?

Earthquakes can strike any location at any time. But history shows that they occur in the same general patterns year after year, principally in three large zones of the earth. The world's greatest earthquake belt, the Circum-Pacific seismic belt, is found along the rim of the Pacific Ocean, where about 81 percent of the world's largest earthquakes occur. It has earned the nickname 'Ring of Fire'. The belt extends from Chile, northward along the South American coast through Central America, Mexico, the West Coast of the United States, and the southern part of Alaska, through the Aleutian Islands to Japan, the Philippine Islands, New Guinea, the island groups of the Southwest Pacific, and to New Zealand. This earthquake belt was responsible for 70,000 deaths in Peru in May 1970, and 65 deaths and a billion dollars damage in California in February 1971.

The second important belt, the Alpide, extends from Java to Sumatra through the Himalayas, the Mediterranean and out into the Atlantic. This belt accounts for about 17 percent of the world's largest earthquakes.

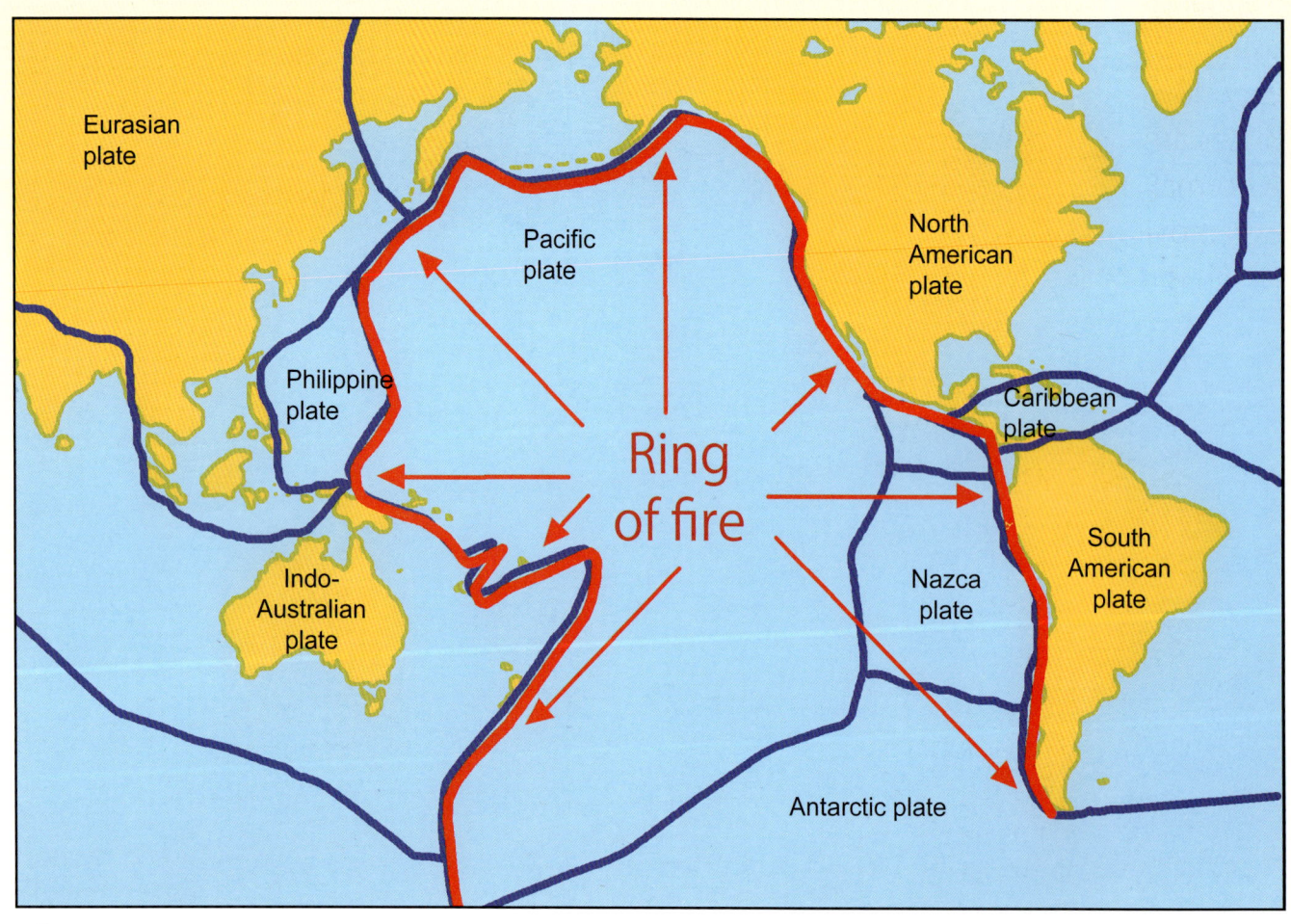

What is a fault?

Large earthquakes can occur on the boundaries where two plates meet, but they are not limited to these areas. As the plates move, fractures in the earth's crust develop and earthquakes are often located on them. These fractures are referred to as faults, of which there are three types and all generate earthquakes when they move.

Types of faults

Normal faults

Normal faults is a dip-slip fault where one block of rock slides downward and away from another block of rock. These faults usually occur in areas where a plate is very slowly splitting apart or where two plates are pulling away from each other. A normal fault is defined by the hanging wall moving down relative to the footwall, which is moving up.

> It was recognized as early as 350 BC by the Greek scientist Aristotle that soft ground shakes more than hard rock in an earthquake.

Reverse faults

Reverse faults are cracks formed where one plate pushes into another plate. They also occur where a plate is folding up because it's being compressed by another plate pushing against it. At these faults, one block of rock is sliding underneath another block or one block is being pushed up over the other. A reverse fault is defined by the hanging wall moving up relative to the footwall, which is moving down.

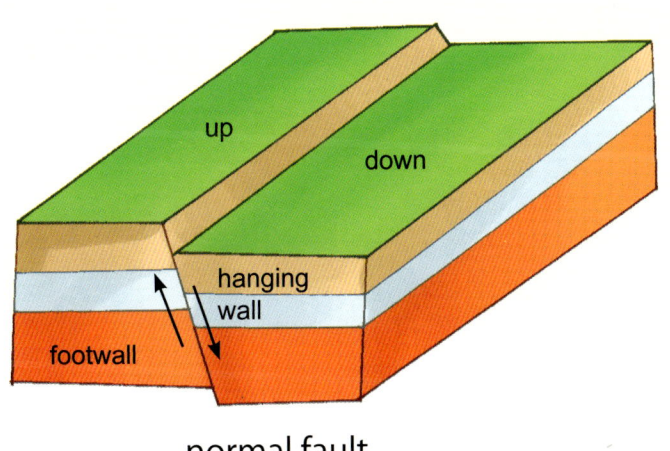

normal fault

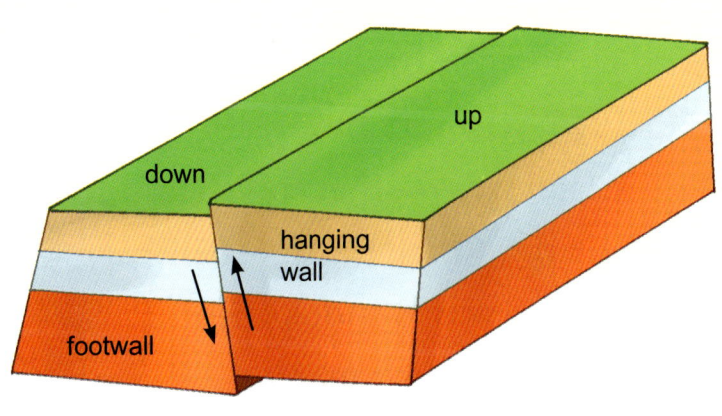

reverse fault

7

Strike-slip faults

Strike-slip faults are the cracks between two plates that are sliding past each other. In a strike-slip fault, two blocks slide past one another. You can find these kinds of faults in California. The San Andreas Fault is a strike-slip fault. It's the most famous California fault and has caused a lot of powerful earthquakes.

San Andreas Fault

strike-slip fault

Astonishing fact

When the Chilean earthquake occurred in 1960, seismographs recorded seismic waves that travelled all around the Earth. These seismic waves shook the entire earth for many days!

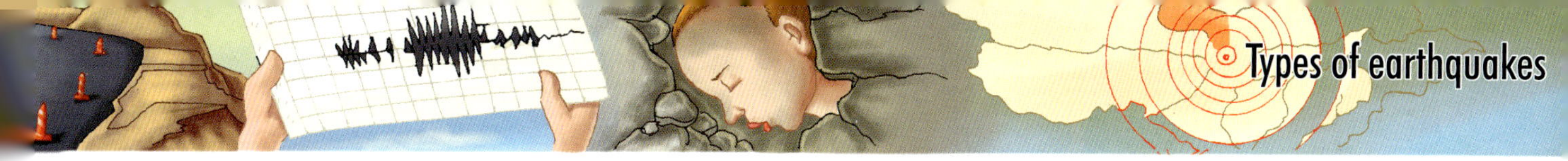

Types of earthquakes

Tectonic earthquakes

The earth's crust consists of loose broken fragments of lands known as the tectonic plates. These tectonic plates have the ability to slowly and gradually move. Now, these plates can move away from each other, towards each other, can collide or can slide past each other.

When the two tectonic plates slide over each other a huge tremor takes place, and that's how a tectonic earthquake occurs.

Tectonic earthquakes are the most common type of earthquake. The tremors caused by tectonic earthquakes are mostly severe and if they are of high magnitude, they can completely destroy a whole city within seconds!

Volcanic earthquakes

Volcanic earthquakes occur when the volcano produces acidic lava. It dries quickly and blocks the top of the volcano so no more magma can escape. Pressure starts to build up and eventually the acidic lava can no longer stand the pressure. So when the volcano explodes, the pressure is released so quickly that an earthquake is caused. A volcanic earthquake happens usually within 16-32kms of the volcano.

Astonishing fact

Earthquakes on the moon are known as 'moonquakes'.

Collapse earthquakes

Collapse earthquakes are comparatively smaller earthquakes and they take place around underground mines.

These earthquakes are also referred to as the 'mine bursts'. The collapse earthquakes are caused by the pressure induced within the rocks. It results in the collapse of the roof of the mine which causes further tremors. Collapse earthquakes are common in small towns near these underground mines.

Explosion earthquakes

The explosion earthquakes are caused due to the nuclear explosions. These man induced earthquakes are one of the biggest side effects of the modern nuclear war.

Astonishing fact

Earthquakes are one of the few natural disasters which is not dependent on the weather. This means that earthquakes can occur in any kind of weather.

In the 1930s, during the American nuclear tests, many small villages and towns suffered through such tremors. Many of them were completely destroyed due to this heinous act.

Aftershocks

Aftershocks occur within the first hour of the main shock of an earthquake, which decreases in magnitude with every subsequent shock. Aftershocks are normally of a lesser magnitude than the main shock of earthquakes and they come in a cluster one after the other after the main shock has stricken. The aftershocks occur very close to the place which is hit by the earthquakes.

The rate of the aftershocks decreases with passing time. Earthquakes of a great magnitude, which have a very devastating effect are also followed by equally powerful aftershocks. Earthquakes are one of the most destructive weather-related disasters and the aftershocks sometimes last till the next day too. It is best to know about the presence of these aftershocks so that the inhabitants of the place hit by an earthquake can be alert beforehand.

Astonishing fact

The largest recorded earthquake in United States was a magnitude of 9.2, which occurred in Prince William Sound in 1964.

Seismic waves

Seismic waves are the waves of energy caused by the sudden breaking of rock within the earth or an explosion. They are the energy that travels through the earth and is recorded on seismographs. Four types of seismic waves are generated when faulting triggers an earthquake. All the seismic waves are generated at the same time, but travel at different speeds and in different ways. **Body waves** penetrate the earth and travel through it, while **surface waves** travel along the surface of the ground.

Primary and secondary waves are body waves. Primary waves (P-waves) travel the fastest and can move through solids and liquids. P waves are also known as compressional waves, because of the pushing and pulling they do. Subjected to a P wave, particles move in the same direction that the wave is moving in, which is the direction that the energy is travelling in. Secondary waves (S-waves) are slower and travel only through solids. S waves move rock particles up and down, or side-to-side or perpendicular to the direction that the wave is travelling in.

Rayleigh and Love waves are the two types of surface waves. Rayleigh wave energy causes a complex heaving or rolling motion, while Love wave energy causes a sideways movement. The combination of Rayleigh and Love waves results in ground heave and swaying buildings. Surface waves cause the most devastating damage to buildings, bridges, and highways.

Surface Waves

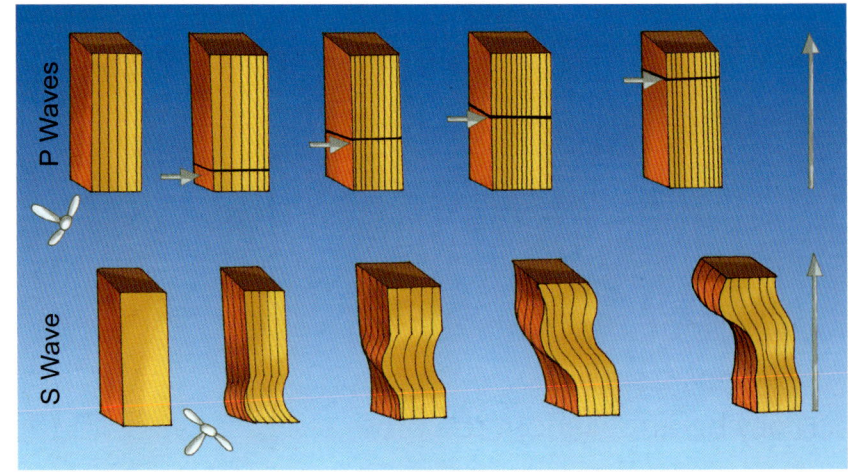

Body Waves

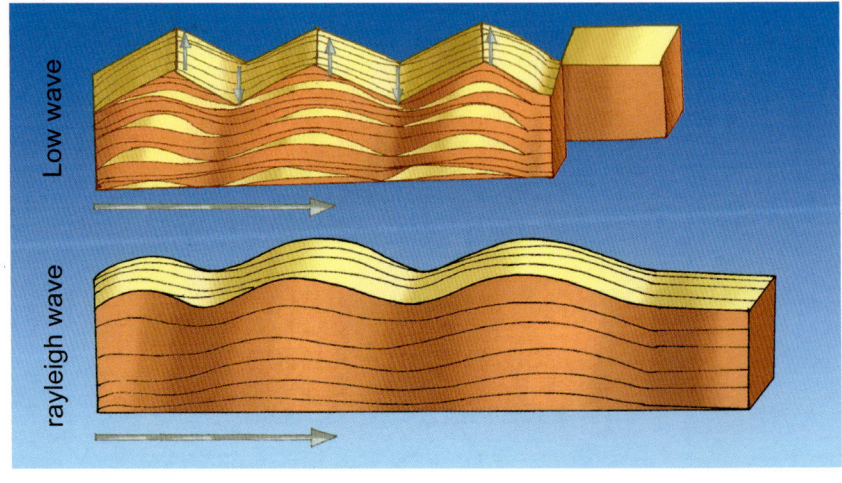

How are earthquakes measured?

Earthquakes are measured in two ways:

- The Richter scale measures the magnitude of an earthquake using an instrument called a **seismograph**. The **Richter scale** is logarithmic, meaning that an earthquake measuring 7 is 10 times more powerful than one measuring 6, and 100 times more powerful than one measuring 5.

- The **Modified Mercalli Scale** is used to measure the intensity of an earthquake in a particular area. It rates each quake from I to XII, depending on how much damage was done.

The point at which an earthquake actually begins, deep below the earth's surface is called the **focus**. If the focus is deep then the effects of the earthquake maybe less as the shockwaves have more rock to move through. Obviously this also depends on what type of rock it is. The point directly above the focus on the earth's surface is called the **epicentre**. The effects of the earthquake are usually worst here, and then radiate out from this spot.

Several thousand stations monitor earthquakes all over the world. Each station contains an instrument, called a seismograph, used to detect arrival times and record seismic waves. The seismograph consists of a **seismometer** (the detector) and a recording device. The seismometer electronically amplifies wave motion.

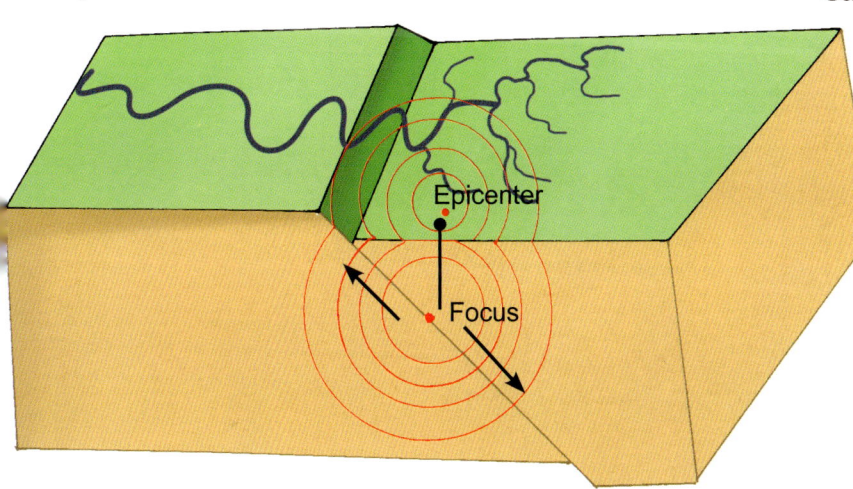

EARTHQUAKES

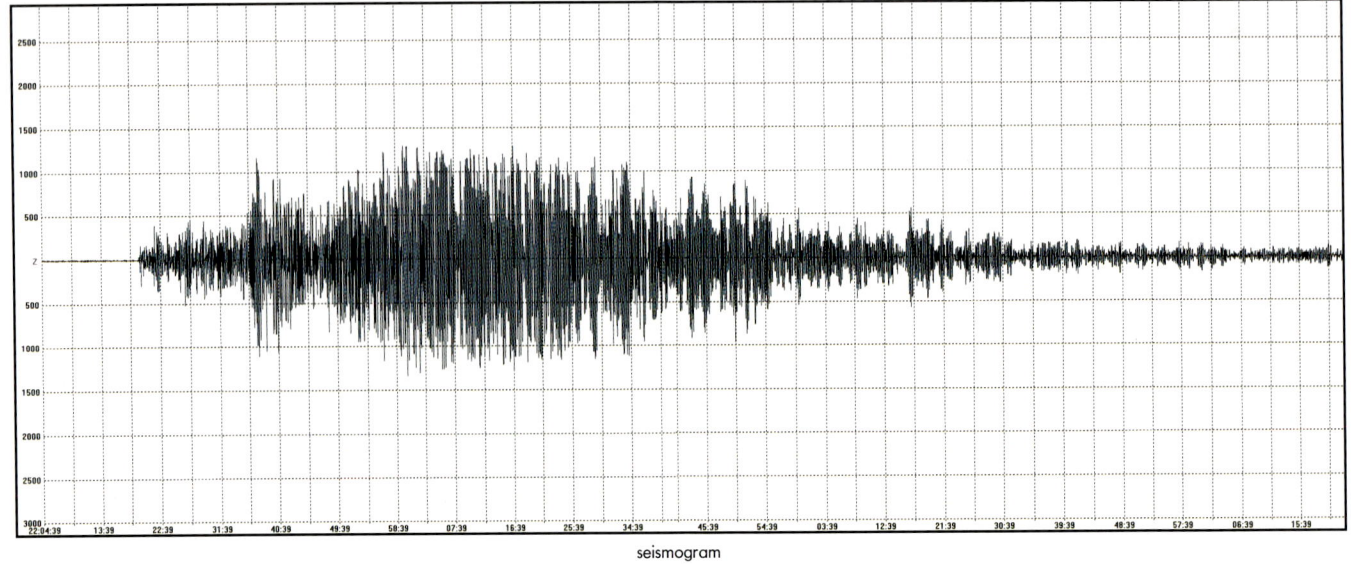
seismogram

The graph on which seismic waves are recorded is called a **seismogram**. The amplitude of the recorded seismic wave is the vertical distance between the crest and trough of the waveform, therefore, the larger the earthquake, the greater the amplitude of the earthquake. The key to locating an earthquake's epicentre is the difference in arrival time, called lag time, of P- and S-waves.

Magnitude and intensity

Earthquakes are categorized in two ways—magnitude and intensity. Magnitude indicates the severity of an earthquake using the Richter scale, a logarithmic, instrumentally determined measurement. Magnitude rates an earthquake as a whole. The Modified Mercalli Scale defines intensity. Intensity is rated by how much damage was caused by an earthquake and how it affected people.

In the San Francisco earthquake of 1906, it is believed that more damage was caused because of the fire after the earthquake than the earthquake itself.

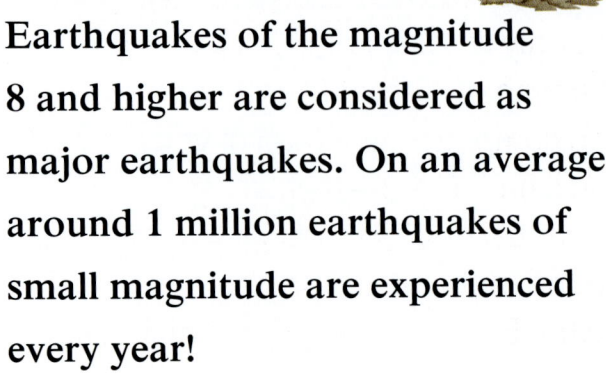

Earthquakes of the magnitude 8 and higher are considered as major earthquakes. On an average around 1 million earthquakes of small magnitude are experienced every year!

Relation between earthquakes and volcanoes

Earthquakes and volcanoes are natural phenomena resulting due to plate tectonics. In general, a volcanic eruption is accompanied by earthquakes.

Earthquakes refer to shaking or trembling of the earth's crust as a result of abrupt release of energy. They are basically seismic waves generated by the natural phenomena or at times, man-made events. Volcanoes, on the other hand are openings in the earth's crust from which hot gases and molten rock materials are ejected on the surface of the Earth.

Earthquakes and volcanoes are related to each other. In fact, earthquakes usually accompany a volcanic eruption. Similarly, unusual earthquakes can lead to volcanic eruptions.

Volcanoes and earthquakes are strongly related. For instance, if you look at a map of earthquakes around the planet and compare it to a map of volcanoes, you'll find that they match closely. Both earthquakes and volcanoes occur at the boundaries of tectonic plates which make up the Earth's surface. Earthquakes are caused by the release of pressure built up when the plates spread apart or move past each or under each other. In slightly more complicated ways, magma is generated at most plate boundaries, and this magma rises to the surface to form volcanoes.

The movement of magma within a volcano causes earthquakes, usually small ones. Earthquakes are also caused by adjustments to the flanks of volcanoes and the plates under volcanoes.

Astonishing fact

Animals can sense or detect earthquakes before they occur.

EARTHQUAKES

Effects of earthquakes

Astonishing fact

There are 500,000 earthquakes around the world each year. 100,000 of those can be felt and only 100 of them cause damage.

Buildings collapsing

People can be trapped in collapsed buildings or under rubble that collapses into the street. This is the type of damage that leads to the worst casualties. The worst thing to do in a quake is to rush out into the street during the quake. The danger from being hit by falling glass and debris becomes many times greater than being inside a building.

In the year 1989 Loma Prieta earthquake, the streets of San Francisco's financial district were covered by broken glass and people were buried under the facade of a brick building that fell forward onto the street. Likewise in the 1964 Alaska earthquake, a huge concrete front wall fell off of a department store onto pedestrians passing by.

Earthquakes produce various damaging effects to the areas they act upon. This includes damage to buildings and in worst cases the loss of human life. The effects of the rumbling produced by earthquakes usually lead to the destruction of structures such as buildings, bridges, and dams. They can also trigger landslides.

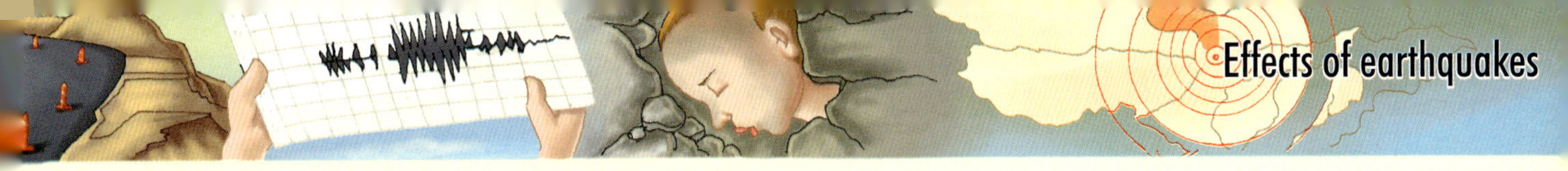

Effects of earthquakes

Buildings knocked off their foundation

Buildings that can otherwise withstand the earthquake can be knocked off their foundations and be severely damaged. This type of damage can be largely prevented by bolting the frame securely to the foundation, so that it will remain in place.

Landslides

Buildings can be damaged when the ground gives way beneath them. This can be in the form of a landslide down a hill, or liquefaction of soils that can cause severe settling of the ground. Ground movement can change the whole landscape, as in the New Madrid Quake that changed the course of the Mississippi River. A landslide into a lake or reservoir can cause flooding downstream. This kind of damage is not unique to earthquakes, but can be triggered by a quake.

> In 1751, primitive seismographs were first built; the reason for the occurrences of an earthquake was determined only in 1855.

landslides

damaged building

EARTHQUAKES

Fire

Fires often break out following earthquakes. They can be caused by flammable materials being thrown into a cooking or heating fire or broken gas lines. Fires can easily get out of control since the earthquake may have broken water mains or blocked roads which firefighters need to use. There are many demands made on the emergency response systems that slow down the response to fires. In the 1906 San Francisco earthquake, for example, the fire that followed the quake caused more damage than the earthquake itself.

tsunami

Tsunami

Underwater earthquakes can produce a tsunami or tidal wave. This wave can travel very rapidly thousands of miles across the ocean. In deep water the tsunami may only raise the ocean level by a few inches hardly enough to notice. But as it approaches land, the shallower water causes the wave to build in height to as much as 15 m or more and suddenly flood the coastal areas. Tsunamis carry a lot of energy and when they hit the coast strong currents can cause massive erosion of the coastline as well as tearing apart buildings it encounters.

fire

Many people believe the lunar cycle influences the earthquakes. However, it is not true because moon never influences earthquakes.

Earthquakes and animals

We can't tell when an earthquake is about to strike, but some people believe other animals can. There have been hundreds of reports of cats, dogs, cockroaches, and rats becoming disoriented and disturbed prior to earthquakes.

In 1975, people reported in north-eastern China mice and rabbits leaving their burrows and snakes coming out of hibernation in the middle of the winter before a huge earthquake occurred.

The night before the big 1906 earthquake, horses in San Francisco grew panicky.

Other sign from animals that an earthquake is coming includes birds flying in circles, dogs barking for hours and elephants starting to run.

The day before the 1964 Good Friday Earthquake, Alaska's Kodiak bears came out of hibernation weeks before schedule.

Better safe than sorry

Earthquake safety tips

- Having knowledge beforehand is the best way to prepare for an earthquake. Here are some easy things to remember when you feel an earthquake happening.

- If you are outside, move away from power lines, trees and buildings.

- If you are inside, stay away from windows, mirrors, cupboards, and shelves.

- Take cover under a sturdy table or desk. Hold on to it.

- You can also stand under a doorway; they are one of the strongest foundations of a house.

- Be prepared for possible shaking after the main earthquake.

- If you are in a high building, stay out of the elevators and stairways.

- A family can prepare for an earthquake by having flashlights, helmets, shoes, a first aid kit, a fire extinguisher, bottled water, canned food and a can opener.

It is estimated that a major earthquake in a highly populated area of the United States could cause as much as $200 billion in losses.

Some deadly earthquakes

The Great Chilean earthquake

The Great Chilean earthquake of May 22, 1960 is the largest magnitude earthquake in recorded history. It measured 9.5 in magnitude and affected southern Chile.

There had been a swarm of earthquakes, as large as magnitude 8, about 160 km to the north the previous day.

Its epicentre was located in Valdivia, approximately 700 kilometres south of Santiago. The earthquake caused a tsunami that ran through the Pacific Ocean and devastated Hilo, Hawaii, 10,000 kilometres from the epicentre, as well as coastal regions of South America. The total number of fatalities from the earthquake/tsunami combination was estimated to have been as many as 3,000.

Despite the record strength of the earthquake, more people were killed by the tsunami than by the earthquake.

EARTHQUAKES

Shaanxi earthquake

The 1556 Shaanxi earthquake or Jiajing earthquake is the deadliest earthquake on record killing approximately 830,000 people. It occurred on the morning of 23 January 1556 AD in Shaanxi, China. More than 97 counties in the provinces of Shaanxi, Shanxi, Henan, Gansu, Hebei, Shandong, Hubei, Hunan, Jiangsu and Anhui were affected. A 520 mile-wide area was destroyed and in some counties, 60% of the population was killed. Most of the population in the area at the time lived in yaodong, artificial caves in loess cliffs, many of which collapsed during the catastrophic occurrence, with great loss of life.

The Shaanxi earthquake occurred during the reign of the Jiajing Emperor of the Ming dynasty. Therefore, in Chinese historical record, this earthquake is often referred as the 'Jiajing Great Earthquake'. While it was the most deadly earthquake and the third deadliest natural disaster in history, there have been earthquakes with higher magnitudes. Aftershocks continued several times a month for half a year. The epicenter was in Hua County near Mount Hua in Shaanxi which is present day Weinan city.

Tangshan earthquake

The Great Tangshan earthquake of July 28, 1976 is one of the largest earthquakes to hit the modern world in terms of the loss of life. The epicenter of the earthquake was near the industrial city of Tangshan in Hebei, China, which housed around one million inhabitants. According to official figures, the earthquake left 242,419 people dead, though some sources estimate it at as many as three times that number. A further 164,581 people were recorded as being severely injured.

The earthquake hit at 3:52 in the morning lasting for around 15 seconds. Many sources list it as 8.2 on the Richter scale. It was followed by a major 7.1 magnitude aftershock some 15 hours later, increasing the death toll.

Many people in Tangshan reported seeing strange lights – so-called 'earthquake lights', the night before the earthquake. In a village outside of Tangshan, well water reportedly rose and fell three times the day before the earthquake. In another village, gas began to spout out the water well on July 12 and then increased on July 25 and July 26. Other wells throughout the area showed signs of cracking.

There is also evidence that the animals had a sixth sense that allowed them to detect the earthquake before it struck. Reportedly, a thousand chickens refused to eat and acted wildly. There were also reports that dogs would not stop barking and even that goldfish jumped out of their bowls!

EARTHQUAKES

Indian Ocean earthquake

The 2004 Indian Ocean earthquake was an undersea earthquake that occurred on December 26, 2004, with an epicenter off the west coast of Sumatra, Indonesia. The earthquake triggered a series of devastating tsunamis along the coasts of most landmasses bordering the Indian Ocean, killing more than 225,000 people in eleven countries, and inundating coastal communities with waves up to 30 meters. It was one of the deadliest natural disasters in history. Indonesia, Sri Lanka, India, and Thailand were hardest hit.

With a magnitude of between 9.1 and 9.3, it is the second largest earthquake ever recorded on a seismograph. This earthquake had the longest duration of faulting ever observed, between 8.3 and 10 minutes. It caused the entire planet to vibrate as much as 1 cm (0.5 inches) and triggered other earthquakes as far away as Alaska. The disaster is known by the scientific community as the Great Sumatra-Andaman earthquake, and is also known as the 'Asian Tsunami' and the 'Boxing Day Tsunami'.

Some deadly earthquakes

Haiyuan earthquake

On December 16, 1920, a huge part of China was rocked by a catastrophic earthquake, the third deadliest earthquake of all time reportedly measuring 7.8 on the Richter scale and claiming over 200,000 lives. The 1920 Haiyuan earthquake occurred in Haiyuan County, Ningxia Province in China at approximately 8pm local time. Measuring as XII or Catastrophic on the Mercalli earthquake intensity scale (the highest possible degree), the Haiyuan earthquake had the intensity causing total damage; lines of sight and level completely distorted with objects thrown into the air and with the ground moving in ripples.

Most of the damage that came from the earthquake was due to landslides. Large-scale landslides occurred on slopes and since the Ningxia Province had numerous slopes and some of them being steep, caused monumental damage. The effect of the 7.8 magnitude earthquake is still on record for being one of the deadliest natural disasters ever recorded. With reported 240,000 lives lost due to the earthquake, the 1920 Haiyuan earthquake is recorded as the 8th worst natural disaster in the history of the world.

EARTHQUAKES

Kanto earthquake

The Great Kanto earthquake was one of the worst natural disasters in the history of mankind and the worst known earthquake in the history of the Japanese islands.

On September 1, 1923 two minutes before noon, a devastating earthquake hit the densely populated area of Tokyo and Yokohama. The shocks reached 7.9 on the Richter scale. The damages caused by the fires that immediately broke out and raged for three days, were by far worse than those caused by the earthquake itself. When the first shocks hit, many charcoal cooking stoves were in use for the preparation of lunch. And light to strong winds made the fires spread within a few minutes in Tokyo and Yokohama.

The death toll was terrible. 140,000 people lost their lives - 58,000 of them in Tokyo. The typical Japanese houses were light buildings with wooden tile roofs and fires had always been a major threat in Japanese cities. Houses were built close to each other with hardly any empty space between them. People had no place to escape and most victims suffocated or burned in the fires. Tokyo and Yokohama were destroyed to 70 and 80 percent.

Ashgabat earthquake

The 1948 Ashgabat earthquake, at a magnitude of 7.3, occurred on 5 October 1948 near Ashgabat, Turkmenistan (then Soviet Union).

The earthquake caused extreme damage in Ashgabat and nearby villages, where almost all brick buildings collapsed, concrete structures were heavily damaged and freight trains were derailed. Damage and casualties also occurred in the Darreh Gaz area, Iran. Surface rupture was observed both northwest and southeast of Ashgabat. Many sources list the casualty total at 10,000, but a news release on 9 December 1988 advised that the correct death toll was 110,000. A 2007 report by the State News Agency of Turkmenistan gives a total number of up to 176,000.

It was this earthquake that killed future Turkmen dictator Saparmurat Niyazov's mother (his father having died during World War II) and the rest of his family, leaving him an orphan.

EARTHQUAKES

Messina earthquake

On the early morning of December 28, 1908, the Italian city of Messina awoke to the deadliest earthquake in European history. Striking just days after Christmas in the Straits of Messina, the 7.2 magnitude quake shook for nearly 30 seconds, toppling several storey buildings and burying alive its occupants. Minutes later, the tsunami came, measuring somewhere between 6-9 m high. The waves were gradually followed by smaller ones, until the water finally subsided.

When the earthquake was over, the city of Messina, with a population of 150,000 had been entirely destroyed. It also destroyed the nearby city of Reggio di Calabria and other outlying areas. It is estimated that the combined earthquake and tsunami killed almost 100,000 people.

Some deadly earthquakes

Lisbon earthquake

The 1755 Lisbon earthquake, also known as the Great Lisbon Earthquake, took place on November 1, 1755, at 9:40 in the morning. It was one of the most destructive and deadly earthquakes in history, killing between 60,000 and 100,000 people. The earthquake was followed by a tsunami and fire, resulting in the near-total destruction of Lisbon.

As the first earthquake studied scientifically for its effects over a large area, it signaled the birth of modern seismology. Geologists today estimate the Lisbon earthquake approached magnitude 9 on the Richter scale, with an epicenter in the Atlantic Ocean about 200 km west-southwest of Cape St. Vincent.

Effects from the earthquake were far reaching. The worst damage occurred in the south-west of Portugal. Lisbon, the Portuguese capital, was the largest and the most important of the cities damaged. Severe shaking was felt in North Africa and there was heavy loss of life in Fez and Mequinez. Moderate damage was done in Algiers and in southwest Spain. Shaking was also felt in France, Switzerland, and Northern Italy. A devastating fire following the earthquake destroyed a large part of Lisbon, and a very strong tsunami caused heavy destruction along the coasts of Portugal, southwest Spain, and western Morocco.

EARTHQUAKES

Haiti earthquake

The 2010 Haiti earthquake was a catastrophic magnitude 7 earthquake centred approximately 25 kilometres from Port-au-Prince, the capital of Haiti, striking on Tuesday, 12 January 2010. The earthquake occurred at a depth of 13 kilometres. The United States Geological Survey recorded a series of aftershocks, fourteen of them between magnitudes 5.0 and 5.9. The International Red Cross estimated that about three million people were affected by the quake, and the Haitian Interior Minister believes that up to 200,000 could be dead, exceeding earlier Red Cross estimates of 45,000–50,000 people killed. A number of prominent public figures are among the dead.

The earthquake caused major damage to Port-au-Prince. Most major landmarks were significantly damaged or destroyed, including the Presidential Palace, the National Assembly building, the Port-au-Prince Cathedral, and the main jail. To compound the tragedy, most hospitals in the area were destroyed.

Test Your MEMORY

1. What is an earthquake?

2. Where do earthquakes occur?

3. Name two causes of earthquakes.

4. Name the three types of faults.

5. Name the types of earthquakes.

6. What is an aftershock?

7. How are earthquakes measured?

8. Write about two damages caused by earthquakes.

9. Write three earthquake safety tips.

10. Name the largest magnitude earthquake in history.

11. Name the deadliest earthquake in history.

12. Write two lines about the Kanto earthquake.

Index

A

aftershocks 2, 11, 22, 32

B

body waves 12

C

circum-pacific seismic belt 6, 32
collapse earthquakes 10
crust 3, 4, 5, 7, 9, 15, 32

D

disruptions 5, 32

E

epicentre 13, 14, 21
explosion earthquakes 10

F

faults 3, 7, 8, 31, 32

I

inner core 4, 32

intensity 13, 14, 25, 32

L

landslide 17, 32

M

magma 5, 9, 15, 32
magnitude 9, 11, 13, 14, 21, 23, 24, 25, 27, 28, 29, 30, 31, 32
mantle 4, 32
modified mercalli scale 13, 14

N

normal faults 7, 32

O

outer core 4, 32

P

plates 3, 4, 5, 7, 8, 9, 15, 32
plate tectonics 4, 15, 32

R

reverse faults 7, 32
richter scale 13, 14, 23, 25, 26, 29, 32
ring of fire 6, 32

S

seismic waves 2, 12, 32
seismogram 14
seismograph 13, 24
seismometer 13
strike-slip faults 8, 32
surface waves 12

T

tectonic earthquake 9, 32
tectonic plates 3, 9, 15, 32
tremors 5, 9, 10, 32
tsunami 18, 21, 28, 29, 32

V

volcanic earthquakes 9